Where I Belong

THE ULTIMATE STEP BY STEP PROCESS OF DECIDING WHAT CAREER TO BREAK INTO

Harwood E. Jones

Where I Belong © 2016 Harwood E. Jones
All Rights Reserved.

Book Description

Are you happy in your current career? Do you plan on being there the rest of your life? What are you doing if it's not? Should you quit or go into business for yourself?

This eye-opening book introduces the readers to the complete crash course of career development basically to the individuals who are working a dead-end job and those who are eager to learn more career development.

The author gives a practical insight, techniques and the actionable steps the reader can apply in career development using the following:

- Asked for relocate-evaluate your current situation
- Create image of your future before finding a new job
- Prepare your resumes for the interview
- Create advancement plan for your promotion
- How to handle workplace conflict
- How to manage difficult coworkers

- Build a productive relationship with your manager

- Why you should not quit your job

If you want to emerge successful in life, pursue your career and the rest of your life plan, read this guide to know how to develop your career, and be focused since in this unpredictable economic time there is every reason not to wait. For those whose dreams are escaping, I give them an actionable advice to try following this guide since it is such a simple guide written in simple language that everybody can easily understand. Go through this manual, take your able body and act immediately.

INTRODUCTION

For any organization, growth is a must which can only be achieved by hard work and determination. If all the resources are not used in a uniform way, then they cannot grow or have profits. In the field of business, all the employees are important and essential so you must give them equal attention. All of them should get equal rights and opportunity to boost their career. It is said that love your work and not your company, which only you can prove wrong by providing great development opportunities to your staff.

If your performance rate is going down, if you are unable to give your full potential, if the environment of your organization has become stale, then you should improve it through career development training. This training is for anyone who is looking to kick start their career. In this training, there will be individual programs to guide you in your career development process.

The underlying problems that are faced by many in the workforce are communication, lack of knowledge, skills, and behavior. With the help of career development training, you can brush up your skills. If you are not proving to be productive for the economy of the company, then arrange for development courses. These courses are given by leading professionals in the field of career development who have enough global exposure. With their knowledge, you can learn new and efficient methods to improve productiveness in your business. You can access a course here (http://soldonsuccess.net/courses/).

Career development training will help in developing the communication between you, your boss, and your coworkers, making the work environment better. Every company has different employees belonging to diverse backgrounds which can come into the way of communication hampering the growth of your productiveness. With the help of this book, you can learn to create a work situation beneficial to you and your wellbeing.

Thank you for purchasing my book, it is my sincere hope it will answer your questions on career development.

Book Description 5

INTRODUCTION 7

Chapter 1: ASKED TO RELOCATE-EVALUATE CURRENT SITUATION BY IDENTIFYING YOUR STRENGTH AND WEAKNESS 10

- How to Identify Your Strengths and Weaknesses 11
- Find Weaknesses 12
- Change the Weaknesses Depending on Your Possibilities 13

Chapter 2: CREAT AN IMAGE OF YOUR FUTURE BEFORE FINDING A NEW JOB 15

- Creating an Action Plan 16

Chapter 3: PREPARING YOUR RESUME FOR THE INTERVIEW 19

- Preparing for the Interview 20
- Assessing yourself 22

Chapter 4: CREATE ADVANCEMENT PLAN BY CHOOSING RESPONSIBILITIES WHICH WILL PROMOTE YOU IN YOUR NEW JOB 24

Chapter 5: HOW TO HANDLE WORK PLACE CONFLICT 27

Chapter 6: HOW TO HANDLE DIFFICULT COWORKERS 29

Chapter 7: BUILD A PRODUCTIVE RELATIONSHIP WITH YOUR MANAGER 33

- Benefits of Having This Strong Relationship 33
- Building Your Relationship With Your Boss 34

Chapter 8: WHY YOU SHOULD NOT QUIT YOUR JOB 37

- CHANGE THE JOB 38
- START YOUR OWN BUSINESS 41

Conclusion 44

Chapter 1: ASKED TO RELOCATE- EVALUATE CURRENT SITUATION BY IDENTIFYING YOUR STRENGTH AND WEAKNESS

Is your current job perfect for you? Are you happy with your career? You need to analyze yourself a lot to provide correct answers here. Lots of people are keeping their current jobs even if they are not happy with them. That's because it's hard to research them to find out how they could influence their career so that they could reach their goals. Of course, they are not totally unsatisfied with their job, but they could never say that they feel happy with it.

It is wrong to consider that the perfect job is always related to money or status. Also, it happens for a lot of people to realize that their "dream job," in reality, is entirely different to what they would have expected.

There are a lot of situations in which people have dropped very well paid jobs for some other jobs which were offering more personal satisfaction. It is paramount for you to work on something you like, you enjoy doing, and you feel accomplished while doing it!

But, to find out what you like the most and when you feel accomplished, you need to search deep inside your soul and, of course, you have, to be honest with yourself while doing this.

Find the answer to the following questions:

A) Am I happy with my work?

B) Can I change something for me to be satisfied with my current work (job)?

If the answer to this question is "No," proceed to the next question:

C) When will I start looking for a new position?

For you to have a clear view regarding your current situation, you need to take into consideration the below-mentioned factors. By doing this, the answers to the questions mentioned above will come easier. In the end, you will know if the current situation of your job fits you, or, on the contrary, you might need to do something about it.

• How to Identify Your Strengths and Weaknesses

It's easy to see where your strengths are. Each time you need to make the next step in your career, you are using your muscles. They are responsible for pushing you forward until your work will be offering enough personal satisfaction.

Some people are good at something, but they are not interested in it. Others are interested in something, but they are not good at doing it. The ideal situation is for people to be good at something they are interested in. You need to find this ideal location and place your strengths will be, too. Your career needs them, and you need them, too, to locate the balance between your personal satisfaction and your motivation.

Some experimented people know very well how good they are at doing something and, also, how interested they are in doing that thing. It means that they know in what area their strengths are.

However, it is always an excellent idea to ask for feedback from other people regarding their opinion on your strengths. Identify the colleagues and friends which could provide you with this kind of feedback and, also, think of some leaders you had during your career and ask them to do a performance review in which your strengths should be highlighted. The ideas received from all of these people will form an excellent source of information when it comes to identifying your strengths.

It is imperative to know your weaknesses, too. That's because, when you are following your career path towards your goal, your weaknesses could be a serious roadblock. Therefore, knowing them before starting with this track will help you eliminate all this kind of obstacles.

You can consider a weakness that area where your actual capabilities are not by the minimum requirements of a particular job. There are a lot of examples of flaws: some people don't have enough knowledge to do a particular job, they are not compatible with the work environment or, simply, they have insufficient technology expertise to fulfill some job requirements.

If you plan to change your job or to proceed with the next step in your career, you may often find out that there is a competition between you and other people which are trying to obtain the same position. It is possible for them to have a better education and knowledge than you and, of course, they will have higher chances to secure the position you are targeting. Therefore, you need to take care of this possible weakness you might have.

In the same manner described above, some people could better cope with a particular working environment, compared to you. This is another significant weakness that many people have. Make sure you don't have it while trying to create your ideal career path.

A significant weakness which could severely lower your chances of obtaining the position you want, and advance on your career path, is the old technology knowledge.

Apparently, you cannot leave your weaknesses as they are. To act upon them, you need to follow a simple process:

• **Find Weaknesses**

As with identifying strengths, finding your weakness is a process in which you might have to search deep inside you and, also, you could need to ask others to provide you with feedback: your colleagues and your leader, too.

In which regards your weaknesses, your colleagues could have a different opinion than you. You should ask some of your appropriate partners to provide feedback regarding your weaknesses.

Your leader could provide one of the best feedbacks regarding your weaknesses. That's because, during performance reviews, your boss is assessing this side of you very carefully. You can just contact your manager and ask his/ her opinion regarding your weaknesses. Of course, make sure this meeting will not impact the business because it will surely be needed about 60 minutes for this kind of conversation.

During the conversation with your boss, you should remember the following advice:

- First, let him/ her know the reason for asking this kind of discussion. Inform your manager that you are doing this because you want to improve your career and establish a correct career path which will take you to the goals you have set. Weaknesses are an important piece of your strategy, and his/ her point of view is very pertinent here.

- If some of your leader's statements are not clear for you, just ask for examples.

- If you disagree with some of your manager's points of view, don't try to defend yourself. Remember that, in this current situation, criticism is what you are looking for. Of course, you can try to present your opinion regarding these critics in the future.

- At the end of the meeting, you should thank your manager for taking the time to discuss with you and let him/ her know that this meeting has helped you in your self-development process and you are trying to cover all your weaknesses that have been highlighted during this session.

• Change the Weaknesses Depending on Your Possibilities

Remember, that it is never an easy task to accept your weaknesses. But, at the same time, it is almost impossible to plan your career without knowing in which area you have to improve yourself. It is also a good idea to make a plan on how you will remedy your weaknesses.

You should be able to correct the flaws in your soft skills area: communication skills, interacting skills, delegation, etc. There are courses which address these shortcomings and help you improving in this area. [Here are some areas](http://soldonsuccess.net/4-areas-invest/#more-77))to begin with.

Weaknesses regarding hard skills can be corrected, too. If for example, your technical knowledge is not very good, you could always find support in specialized training which has been designed for this kind of capability. Remember that you could find on the internet a lot of free support for the technical matters.

Chapter 2: CREAT AN IMAGE OF YOUR FUTURE BEFORE FINDING A NEW JOB

During almost each job interview there is one question which cannot miss: Where do you see yourself in 5 years? If you don't have a very clear answer to this question, then you have not created the image of your future. It is dangerous, because you risk having your career path blocked by a job in which you cannot advance, and your level of dissatisfaction will grow a lot.

However, don't forget the following when creating the image of your future:

- Take into consideration your values, interests, skills, lifestyle, strengths, and weaknesses

- Remember that your choices could change over time. Therefore don't stick too much to a particular job type

- Focus on the entire picture instead of just on some details. It means that your primary goals should be priority and other unimportant things should be left aside

It often happens to us, when we are thinking about our future, to come up with some questions which are meant to stimulate our thinking. Try to remember those issues. They could sound like this:

-What is the activity that I enjoy doing the most?

When you are doing something that you like, chances are your performances to be at their best.

-What kind of job could perfectly fit me?

It is important for you to be interested in doing a particular kind of job. Again, the results on that job will be at a higher level.

-What kind of industry could attract me the most?

If for example, you are drawn to cars, you should investigate the automotive sector and find out if your competencies fit the requirements of a job in this area. If they are, then you should guide your career path towards this industry, because employment in this field could offer more satisfaction compared to one in the insurance field.

Don't forget to investigate the jobs market and find out if the job of your dreams exists. In this way, you will know, also, what is the industry that will provide you with this job. Now, your image about the future will look more realistic.

While looking for that particular field which could offer you enough satisfaction, it is a good idea to reverse, for the moment, the logical thinking: try to identify how your skills, interests, and strengths could be useful for an individual domain of activity.

As mentioned above, don't stick too much with a particular "dream job." Some changes might appear in your life, career or on the jobs market. It is always wise to anticipate those changes and have a backup plan for each of them. The image of your future must be ready to support these changes and updates, too.

If, after the researchers mentioned above, you figure out that you might not be the right person for the job or industry you are aiming, obviously you have to look in other industries or markets. Don't forget that the online environment is a very useful resource of information. Furthermore, it is recommended that you access sites where networks of online friends are sharing information about their careers. Try to add as many contacts as you can. Your chances of finding a job or industry that fits you correctly are growing a lot when using this kind of networks.

• Creating an Action Plan

The next step, after creating the image of your future, is the designing of an action plan. Because your career path is like a road, you need to use a map to navigate correctly on it and avoid dead-ends or other paths which will take you to places you don't want.

The action plan you will be creating shall contain the goals and the objectives that will guide you towards the image you have created, as described in the previous sub-chapter.

A good idea, when designing your action plan, is to divide it into several pieces and start with the beginning.

If you are familiar with the annual performance review, then designing an action plan for your career should be easy.

You are reading a lot in this e-book about goals and objectives. They are paramount because, without them, you will not be able to monitor your advance through your career path. Also, they are helping a lot with constantly remembering the image of your future.

The goals and objectives which you embed in your action plan will lead you towards the qualifications needed for your future jobs, will provide you with an excellent vision of your progress on the path you have selected and will also provide you with a great feeling of motivation.

The intermediary points, as described in the paragraphs mentioned above, should be periods of time when you are trying to update/ improve your skills and capabilities. Also, all your knowledge gaps should be covered in these intermediary phases of your action plan. Some of these shortcomings could be covered through training. For other gaps, training might not be enough. You should also concentrate on gathering experience in that particular domain.

Look for training inside the company/ industry you are already part of. Extend your research towards specialized organizations (like universities, specialized schools, etc.) Don't forget that you can find a lot of online training. They could be more comfortable and, why not, cheaper.

Finding training was the easy part. Gaining experience is a little bit more difficult. And that's because most of the employers are reticent when it comes to hiring people without expertise in a particular field. But, don't worry…there are quite a few solutions: voluntarism, internships, job shadowing, temping, etc. The best part about these solutions is that they allow you to figure out if the job of your dreams is, in fact, the one that you want. This is possible because you see with your own eyes what does a particular job requires you to do.

As you might already have noticed, one of the scopes of creating a career plan is to highlight the training and job experience, which you need to reach your career goals.

Chapter 3: PREPARING YOUR RESUME FOR THE INTERVIEW

If you can't be that detail orientated that you take the time to personalize your resume, and then are you the best person for the job? In my time, I have come across some pretty unimpressive resumes. Some candidates were obviously over-qualified while others were so skimpy with the information that they looked apathetic toward getting the job. Some were handwritten and poorly written too, while others were typed out with mistakes all over the place and they hadn't even bothered to make an effort to make the resume look impressive.

You can never tell until you meet someone how suitable they are going to be for a job, but if your resume sucks, then you may not even get as far as an interview. Your education is important and your previous employment, but if you worked in a holiday camp while you were a student, don't use that unless it is relevant to the job. It does not really work unless it's related to what you are being asked to do in the new job. You can add this in your personal interest area as something that you do, because it may be relevant to the social side of the work that you are applying for.

Think of all the things that are of interest to the job. For example, if you know that you are under qualified, up the ante by adding what makes you think that you are suited to work in question. You may be competing with graduates that have the qualifications but not the common sense. By adding some requirement of why you think you can do the job, you may just hit the right note that gets you past the door for the interview. Employers know that some qualified people are very good at passing exams but not much use in a day to day situation. It depends on the business how strictly they enforce their qualification rules.

You should put your name at the top of the resume and your address. The reason for this is that it may become detached from your letter and if the employer doesn't have your address, it's not likely that you will hear from them. Your telephone number, your mobile, and your email address are vital.

Then add something unique. Insert the name of the company to which you are applying and the job you are applying for. It personalizes your resume and makes it look like it was tailored for the job you are applying for.

Educational qualifications come next, and here you shouldn't overdo it. If you have a degree in sociology and you are applying for a job as a shop manager, it may not be that impressive. The qualifications which are relevant should be the ones that get into the spotlight. You can add the others, but also add that these were taken at a time when you were unsure of your future and were good from a discipline point of view in that they taught you the importance of the study.

As far as the jobs go, if you have little experience, try to avoid listing jobs that are irrelevant. Instead of doing that, fill this section out with what duties you have done in the past that are relevant. For example, you may have been a team leader in something unrelated, but team-leading may be essential to the job that you are applying for. Try to make every bit of your resume relevant because it is and believe it or not, those who have totally irrelevant resumes and who haven't bothered to personalize them may be hitting the reject pile for that reason.

When sending in a resume, you must remember to write a letter to go with it. It shows that you have taken the time to make an effort. Your handwriting should be legible and if your handwriting does let you down, type the letter but make sure that you sign it with a pen so that it doesn't look like a photocopied letter sent to many people. Attention to detail is so important.

• **Preparing for the Interview**

If that means sneaking downtown and standing outside their offices for half an hour at lunchtime, then it's a good ploy because you won't turn up overdressed and you won't turn up underdressed. Look at the standard of dress of employees because that gives you information that is useful to you.

[You should always be dressed for the part.](http://soldonsuccess.net/dressing-drives-perception-change-youre-perceived/#more-97)

Your shoes should be clean. Your nails need to be clean and well cared for. Each of the little things that people look forgives them information about your character. What you look like counts for a lot. The fact that you made an effort is a great thing, but do you know what you look like to others? Have you taken a look at how you enter a room, how you shake hands with people and how you appear when you sit down?

Body language is everything in an interview. Certain behaviors don't do you any justice, and you need to learn to overcome bad habits that you may have acquired. It doesn't cross some people's minds, but believe me; body language will get you rejected if it's as negative as it was in some interviewees that I interviewed. The kinds of behaviors to look out for are:

➢ Limp handshakes – These show insecurity and sometimes insincerity

➢ Playing with your ring finger – This shows impatience

➢ Not looking the interviewer in the eye – This shows potential deception

➢ Wriggling in your seat – This shows extra nervousness

➢ Looking downward – This shows you have something to hide

➢ Slouching – This shows a lazy tendency

On top of these habits, you also have speech patterns which are very irritating and which may stop you from getting the job. Look at the patterns below, and if you are guilty of any of them, you need to practice to get out of the habits because they are not what interviewers are looking for:

- The use of slang and bad language

- Interrupting when someone is speaking

- Using "um" between words or having a speech habit

Of course, people are not biased against those who have a speech impediment from birth, but if you are applying for a job where your address matters, such as being in touch with clients, you do need to give an open dialog that shows that you are capable of this.

• Assessing yourself

Dressed ready for an interview, walk into your bedroom and see yourself in a full-length mirror. It's best to place a chair in front of the mirror at a distance which is reasonable and watch yourself walk into the room and sit down. Look at your body language and try to correct those things which give all the wrong messages.

Imagine yourself saying "Hello" to the interviewer. Have your head held high, look the interviewer in the face and hold out your hand to shake theirs.

Practicing your sitting position with a mirror makes you very aware of things that may be seen by a potential interviewer. For example, are your pants too short and reveal your badly chosen socks? If you are a woman, are you revealing anything that you should not be when you are seated? Look for what someone else sees by watching yourself in the mirror. The way that you walk, the way that you hold your head and the way that you take your seat are all being noticed by strangers. If you are not happy with any of these, go out of the room and practice again.

It is particularly relevant to women who try to wear heels that are uncomfortable. Do you think that a company wants a woman who wobbles on her heels and who shows a lack of confidence? Of course not.

Change those shoes because confidence is what you need to display at an interview. Is your skirt too short and giving the wrong impression? It is an interview. It's not a good way to get a job, particularly if the interviewers are older women who don't have the body that you do. You may even find that they are naturally biased against you because you appear so sexy. That may sound a little severe, but believe me, if there are older women on the panel that interviews you; you need their approval to get the job.

Chapter 4: CREATE ADVANCEMENT PLAN BY CHOOSING RESPONSIBILITIES WHICH WILL PROMOTE YOU IN YOUR NEW JOB

Even if you have setup everything that the career path requires, there is still some effort required from your side. Things are just happening if you don't make them happen. Therefore, it is always recommended that you constantly search for opportunities inside the company you are already working for.

The following steps need to be accomplished when you decide to find another position inside your organization:

A. Look for new posts and opportunities. To accomplish this first step, you need to take into consideration the followings:

- Nowadays organizations are advertising all the new job opportunities internally. Constantly check for these new opportunities and target the ones that might fit your requirements.

- Some of the organizations have inside job changing regulations. For example, if you had already changed your position a couple of months ago, you might not be able to change it again until the end of the fiscal year.

- After identifying a position that might suit your expectations, try to consult with people that are already working on this particular location and ask for feedback. You need to find out if you are the correct person for this kind of job and, also, if this area will meet your personal requirements.

B. Look for self-development opportunities. As already described in this e-book, your skills and competencies need to be permanently updated and improved. Most of the companies are offering all kind of resources for this scope, and you need to use them. These are the most frequent training that you could find in each company's training curricula: certifications, management, leadership, different tools or software which is used in various areas. From time to time, various organizations are offering training programs for their employees. Always check what your company has to offer for you to grow your knowledge, and make sure you use these opportunities to (or "intending to") develop yourself and improve your chances to advance on your career path.

Besides the obvious opportunities which are coming from the above-described direction, some other "not so evident" benefits will appear: you will show that your interest in self-developing is at a very high level; you are proactive; you might gain more trust from your managers.

C. Look, also, for lateral moves inside your company. It can be done in the department you are already working right now, too.

If your new career path is in another area of the organization, you should not fear to consider a "downgrade" of your job, if the new one is using more efficiently your skills, capabilities, interests and it is fitting better with your requirements and lifestyle.

Benefits: your work experience and expertise will grow; you will meet new people, and you will have new connections, which might help you move forward on your career path; you will have the chance to understand better how a company is organized.

Before deciding to make a lateral move, you need to identify the exact reasons behind this decision (a new opportunity, the location of the new job provides you with some benefits, the career growth is likely to appear faster, etc.). Then, you need to take into consideration your company's policy regarding lateral moves: there might be some restrictions regarding lateral moves inside your organization (e.g.: new employees are allowed make a lateral move only after one year of working in a particular position).

If you wonder why is always important to request new responsibilities at your job, you should know that they will help you building new skills or refresh the ones you already have. You will gain new work experience in a slightly different area and, perhaps, the most significant benefit, you will be observed by the top management and considered a proactive employee.

The key to this process is to ask for these new responsibilities. However, this is not quite simple as it sounds. Naturally, you cannot just demand your manager to provide you with new responsibilities. Therefore, some strategies will need to be used:

- As soon as a new opportunity appears, make sure you are the first to demand it. To be the first one to act when a new responsibility appears, you have to take into account several ideas: always be prepared and aware of the tasks that may come up (try to anticipate them). Try to synchronize with them; don't analyze too much the situation; always think proactively.

It needs to be done after accomplishing being selected as a potential responsibility owner. This clear image of your accomplishments will help you convincing your manager to provide you with this responsibility. Market yourself!

- Do your best to prove your manager that you perform excellently with the new responsibilities that you have been provided with. Even more, you have to show your manager that the new responsibility fits better with your profile when compared to the job/position you already have. To accomplish this goal, you need to highlight those skills and values that your current position does not allow you to use them. Apparently, the new responsibility will make use of them. Of course, this doesn't mean that you should describe the current position as suitable for you. Remember that the new responsibility is not yours, for the moment.

Chapter 5: HOW TO HANDLE WORK PLACE CONFLICT

Have you been having problems at work, namely problems with your boss or your coworkers? If you have, you are not alone. Workplace conflicts are a lot more common than you may have originally thought. You and many others may have problems with a coworker, a supervisor, or both. When faced with a workplace conflict, you will want to be careful, as your actions can have consequences.

When it comes to handing workplace conflicts, there are a number of different factors that you will want to take into consideration. One of those factors is the situation or who you may have a conflict with. If your conflict is with a coworker, you may want to speak with one of your supervisors. On the other hand, if you are having a conflict with your supervisor, you may be able to go above their head and deal with another member of management.

Speaking of having workplace conflicts with a coworker, it is important to note that you need to proceed with caution, especially when reporting their behavior to your supervisor. You need to remember that even the best of workplaces have cliques. You will want to make sure that your supervisor isn't close with the person in question. Even if a relationship does exist, you can still take your concerns to your boss, but you just need to do so in a pleasant and professional way. You will want to avoid, at all costs, sounding like you ate spiteful or gossiping. On the other hand, if you have a problem or a workplace conflict with your supervisor, you will want to consider going above their head, especially if the conflict you are having is a major one.

Major conflict can involve unfair treatment, unpaid overtime, and so forth. Unless you are dealing directly with the owner of your company, you will likely find that your supervisor has a boss and so on. When speaking with a supervisor, especially one who is ahead of your own manager, you will be as professional as possible. You will want to try and schedule a meeting in person. You may have to make arrangements over the phone or through email, but you should refrain from divulging too much information at first. As previously stated, it is important that you are professional when handling any workplace conflict. It may be a good idea to keep documentation of all the complaints or problems you would like to bring attention to. For example, you may want to write down the time and date and a summary of what happens each time that you may be harassed, even if it is not sexual in nature. You will want to have documented proof to back up your claims, especially the serious ones. The last thing that you want to do in a meeting with your supervisor or even their supervisor is come off as unprofessional or as the one with the issues.

    The above mentioned methods are just a few of the many ways that you can go about trying to resolve any conflicts that you may be having at work. Any small issues, such as a coworker wearing a strong perfume, should try to be handled privately first. If you are unable to see success, especially after supervisors have been alerted, you may then want to consider seeking employment elsewhere, but use this only as a last resort.

Chapter 6: HOW TO HANDLE DIFFICULT COWORKERS

Conflict is an everyday occurrence of interacting with other people. You should know that the cost of resolving a conflict is practically nonexistent compared to leaving them unresolved.

Conflicts arise between people in an organization every day, between organizational components or even between institutions. Dealing with conflict has become a part of your job duties. There have been numerous studies suggesting that between 30 and 40 percent of a manager's daily activities consist of solving some kind of interpersonal conflict. If a manager fails to solve these conflicts, it may result in high loss of productivity on the work environment. Ultimately, having a negative impact on others working there.

Adverse behavior can decrease performance in others and will become worse and worse over time if left alone. It will contaminate the whole workplace atmosphere. It takes many forms such as rudeness, yelling, gossiping, don't talking or acknowledging your peers, complaining indefinitely to your supervisors and slowing work.

You might feel that you are being treated unfairly, emotionally abused, discriminated, sexually harassed, anger hostility, cultural diversity and even potential physical and psychological violence! Having to go through these conflicts without sufficient knowledge on how to solve them, the distress might get out of control. It is important to understand how to face these workplace problems effectively.

Let's first discuss how does a conflict start. Most conflicts within a company occur due to unfulfilled needs. These needs are highly linked to human's psychological needs of control, recognition, respect and affection. These affect much more deeply in any human being than something more mundane as they are closely related to the psyche. We should try not to reinforce difficult behavior or actions. There is really no easy way to solve this. It takes a lot of time and patience to change these negative characteristics. You shouldn't ignore this behavior but neither you should criticize or respond similarly to it. The whole work community can work together to prevent these behaviors that leads to a conflicted workplace.

A basic problem in communications is the conflict within each person's desires, concerns, fears and needs. Two coworkers might be discussing why one of them is such a perfectionist in everything he does. One is tired of the other thinking he is always right. Conflict will occur if not solved. One of them feels might feel threatened by the other one because he fears competition with the other one, who is more skilled in doing his job. The other worker might not know what he is doing wrong, or that the other person feels threatened by him. He thinks he is just doing a good job.

When a coworker feels that his job is on the line due to a "perfectionist" he feels intimidated leading to hostility. These two people will become locked in conflict. Closer examining the problem, we can clearly understand that both of them want job stability and a good relationship within each other. But their positions damage their relationship. How can we solve something like this? First off, try to identify the other person's interest. Put yourself in his/her shoes and think what he/she is thinking. You will come with a good solution.

Another cause of conflict might be misunderstanding a problem. Everyone starts taking sides, getting angry and taking things personally just by bad communication. They might feel that a problem is affecting them just by hearing incomplete facts and comments and then inferring certain facts about it. All of these happen due to bad communication. That's why we need to discuss each other's problems and be open about them.

Listening to each other is really important. Try actively listening, paying deep attention of what the other person is saying. You might identify a problem before it has even started and work towards solving it. For listening appropriately, try not to interrupt or argue. Be truly open to the other person's point of view. Be empathetic.

Every time you act empathetically, listening to the other what the other person is saying you understand them much more.

Listening well is often silent, try to absorb like a sponge as much of what the other person is saying. Pay attention to them.

Effective communication is not achieved by taking turns talking, but by a connection and understanding. If you work enthusiastically to understand the other person, giving them feedback and confirmation until the other person has no doubt you care about his point of view. He will feel understood and he will be much more open to hear your problems as well as preventing conflict.

Emotions play a very important role in our behavior. There is no action does is not justified by an emotional counterpart. We often disguise our negative emotions because we are conditioned to do so. No matter how much we disguise them, these emotions show themselves in your actions. An example is a coworker who might become angry and instead of showing his anger, he might just hide this feeling and take a sick day home. Throughout our whole lives we are not completely honest with our feelings. A good way to change this problem of repressing feelings is by talking and having the confidence within each other to express ourselves. Be open and talk about what you are feeling. These will minimize conflicts and problems.

Some simple principles to deal with difficult behavior:

- **Think of conflict as something natural**
People working together have different perceptions. It is only natural that they will disagree in something. Solving these conflicts is a good opportunity to improve communication and build trust between coworkers. Remember to not avoid or hide your problems. Be open and solve them!
- **Cool off and think about the problem** The most common thing to do when dealing with a problem is to face it as soon as it occurs. Give yourself some time with the pillow and think it off.
- **Remember about the other person's feelings** help the other person think about their feelings by listening. Encourage him to speak about their negative feelings.

- **Attack the problem, not the individual** detach the problem from the individual, focus on solving the problem. Try to see the problem from their point of view.
- **Communicate directly** be clear about what you say. Use body language to show support and attention. Ask questions that may solve problems. Be aware of your tone of voice.

Holding onto resentment you have worked with punishes you, them, and everyone around you. You can't change relationships but you can control other people behavior by changing how you interact with them. Listening and showing respect to the people we work with fortifies our relationships. Preventing conflicts between you and your peers.

Chapter 7: BUILD A PRODUCTIVE RELATIONSHIP WITH YOUR MANAGER

The specialists advise that the relationship between our boss and us is paramount for our career.

This link (http://soldonsuccess.net/category/networking-and-communication/) will provide you with value and support when it is time to move forward and, in the same time, it will also create a healthy environment where you can perform in your current role. If you feel that you struggle with building relationships because of your shy personality, here are some ways you still can and be who you are.

Once, your relationship has been set up, you need to take care of it and, also, improve it.

Therefore, this chapter will provide you with valuable information regarding the relationship between you and your manager, advising on the ways of maintaining and making it productive: demonstrating your devotion, offering your support, keeping your manager informed, delivering feedback, etc.

• Benefits of Having This Strong Relationship

The first benefit of having this healthy relationship with your boss is related to your current job. By creating this "connection" with your manager, it is more likely that your work environment will become pleasant and allow you to perform better. Imagine that coming to work will be more like a pleasure and not an obligation. It will allow you to have better results, which, on the long term, translates into a better career path.

This healthy relationship will create a sort of chain reaction: your manager will communicate better with you and provide more accurate expectations. Therefore, you will better understand your tasks and meet your goals faster and more efficiently.

Another important aspect of this healthy relationship is related to your career: your advancement possibilities will grow. That's because it is not enough to work hard, possess the appropriate skills and capabilities and develop the right career path. You also need your manager to notice all of the above and be ready to promote you.

Also, the good relationship between you and your manager provides the benefit of receiving good feedback for your next job. Your next manager is more likely to accept you when your current boss "gives his/ her word" for you.

• Building Your Relationship With Your Boss

To develop this relationship, you need to understand that your boss is human, too. I know it sounds strange and…common. But, most of us tend to forget this important aspect.

Why am I saying this? Well, that's because humans have emotional needs and the managers are no exception from this rule.

You need to show them that you help/ support them and, at the same time, you are loyal. Another, crucial way of building this relationship is by showing your boss that you care and you are ready to help him/ her succeed. In this way, you will receive the same kind of aid when you need most.

Prove that you are devoted. Think that you always appreciate the loyalty of other people. You hate when somebody talks badly about you. Also, you are grateful to people that offer their help when you need it. Your manager thinks the same. Prove him that you are devoted, you are not spreading bad rumors about him/ her, you are ready to offer your support and your relationship with your boss will be a healthy one.

To prove that you are devoted, you can use the following three strategies:

- Create a good image of your boss in the eyes of his/ her managers

- If you can help your boss to accomplish a particular task which has to be done specifically by him/ her, offer your support, without demanding any credit. It is a perfect way of showing that you are loyal because you prove that you care about your manager's goals and achievements, too. You also need to take into consideration that, by letting others know how much of your boss's work is being done by you, will have an adverse impact on your relationship, and, in the end, on your advancement possibilities

- Prove that you respect the chain of commands. When other managers delegate you to accomplish different tasks, inform your direct manager, too. It will let him/ her know that you are loyal. When you have a problem with your boss, don't ask for help from other managers. Just have an honest discussion with him/ her. If you don't respect this last advice, your boss will not look excellent in the eyes of his/ her colleagues.

Reveal your support. Remember how good it feels when your manager encourages you for working on a particular project or congratulates you for achieving precise results? Well, the same he/she feels when you reveal your appreciation towards him/ her. It will, also, strengthen your relationship.

Therefore, the golden rule here is to say some beautiful words to your boss at the right moment. It is also a good idea to say these nice things when you are asked to share your opinion about your manager to other people in your company.

However, don't forget that it is not recommended to exaggerate with showing your appreciation towards your manager. The beautiful words mentioned above must be honest and should come from inside you! They also have to be somehow limited. Otherwise, their effect will be negative, and your boss will not consider your opinions. Also, you need to pick the right moment for showing your appreciation. Usually, it is best to do this at the time when your manager has done something that needs your appreciation. Showing it later will not have the same effect.

Remember to say "Thank You" once in a while. It is the simplest and effective way of showing appreciation towards someone.

Offer your support for your boss to succeed. Sometimes, your targets are your manager's goals, too. Fulfilling your tasks accurately is a performance indicator on which your boss is evaluated. Therefore, make sure you always accomplish your tasks correctly and on due time. But that's not all. You also need to show him/ her that you care and you are ready to offer your support for him/ her to be able to succeed. Think smart and anticipate your manager's needs, give appropriate advice when you are asked and walk that extra mile if this could help your boss succeed.

Take into consideration the following strategies:

- Volunteer. And do this often. That's because your manager needs to know that he/ she can count on you in stressful situations. But remember to do this when it is necessary. Don't exaggerate and volunteer when your help is not required.

- Be proactive. Prevent the happening of different problems. Work smart and anticipate them.

- Give honest feedback to your manager. Don't just say what your boss wants to hear. Provide honest feedback that will help him/ her to better accomplish goals.

Chapter 8: WHY YOU SHOULD NOT QUIT YOUR JOB

Are you frustrated with your job? Whether you dislike your boss, your coworkers, your work hours, or the pay, you may be interested in quitting your job. Of course, the decision to quit your job is your decision to make, but there are some instances in which you may want to give your decision a second thought. Few of those instances are outlined below for your convenience.

One of the many situations where you may want to hold off on quitting your job right away is if you recently got a new boss. If you have a new supervisor, you are encouraged to give it time. Most new supervisors are difficult at first, as they feel that they need to be. But, overtime, you will find that most of those in management will let a new side of themselves show, possibly a more pleasant and friendlier side.

Another one of the many situations in which you may want to reconsider quitting your job is if you are annoyed by one of your coworkers, namely the one who may have a desk or an office next to or near you. You should never let someone else make you quit or lose your job, especially if it is just because you do not like them. Of course, you are advised to take your safety into consideration. If one of your coworkers is displaying actions that may cause you harm, you may need to take action right away. This action may involve resigning from your job, but it should also involve contacting a supervisor first.

You should never have a quit your job because someone else is in the wrong. A poor review is another situation in which you may not want to quit your job. Although it may seem embarrassing and frustrating if you ever receive a bad review, it is important to remember that it can happen to the best of people and the hardest of workers. No one is perfect all of the time and this is something that you need to remember. Instead of quitting your job because of a poor review, you will want to use your review as an opportunity to better yourself. You can set the goal of improving your workplace actions, which should result in a better review the next time around.

Being passed up for a promotion is another reason why you may not want to quit your job. There are a number of different factors to take into consideration, when it comes to promotions, namely being passed up for one. Why were you passed up for the promotion that you wanted? Do you know? Was there another employee who was more qualified or who had more seniority than you? You can also use being passed up for a promotion as a way to improve your work skills by setting goals for yourself. With that in mind, if you regularly find yourself being passed up for promotions that you are more than qualified for, you may want to consider seeking employment elsewhere. The above mentioned situations are all situations in which you may want to refrain from quitting your job, especially without consideration.

Of course, there are extenuating circumstances to the situations mentioned above, such ones that may involve sexual harassment or other dangerous situations in your workplace. Below are two choices you should make before quitting your current job.

• CHANGE THE JOB

Are you currently unhappy with your job or with your employer in general? If you are, you may have considered changing jobs. With that in mind, if you depend on your paycheck to help pay your bills or to help support your family, you may be unsure as to whether or not a job change is really in the best interest of you and your family. If this is something that you have asked yourself before, you will want to continue reading on.

When it comes to determining whether or not you should change jobs, there are a number of important factors that you will want to take into consideration. These factors are important, as no two situations are the same. Different individuals rely on their paychecks for different things. That is why it is advised that you examine the factors outlined below and then use them in your own, personal, situations. One of the many factors that you will want to take into consideration, before deciding if you should change jobs, is your current job's pay. Do you think that you receive a fair salary? If you do, do you know that it may be difficult for you to make the same amount of money elsewhere? Unless you are lucky enough to receive a job in upper level management, you may find yourself right back at the bottom of the ladder, having to work your way right back up. For that reason, you will want to first take your current salary and compare it the salary that is being advertised with job openings that you can find in your local newspapers or online.

Health insurance is another factor that you will want to take into consideration, when deciding if you should change your job. Do you currently rely on your job for health insurance, either for yourself or for your whole family? If you do, this is definitely a factor that needs to be taken into consideration. Yes, you may be able to purchase health insurance for yourself or at least an extension of your coverage, but you should know that this can get quite expensive. With that in mind, should you still decide to switch jobs, you may want to schedule all of your doctor's appointments before you do so, just to get everything in order. If your current coverage includes dental and vision coverage, you may also want to make these appointments too, just in case.

The current job outlook is another factor that you will want to take into consideration. If you are looking to change jobs, do you already have a new job lined up? If you do not, you will want to at least make sure that there is a good chance that you can seek employment elsewhere. In most cases, you are unable to collect unemployment payments if you leave your job on your own terms. If you have a family to support or if you rely on your income to pay important bills, like your rent or mortgage payments, you may want to have a backup plan in place. In keeping with the current job outlook, you are advised to examine all job openings in your area. What you will want to do is examine any required training, work experience, or education. Unfortunately, many individvals realize too late that they are unqualified for their dream job. This is something that you do not want to do. Instead of assuming, you can easily examine the average job requirements by examining all available job openings in your local newspaper or online.

If you do not have the necessary training, you may want to consider enrolling in a career training course, as they may be able to improve your chances of finding a new job. The above mentioned factors are just a few of the many factors that you will want to take into consideration, should you be interested in changing jobs. Of course, the decision to seek employment elsewhere is your decision to make, but, with something this important, you are advised to proceed with caution.

The first question which comes to everybody's mind is related to the motivation for changing the job. It is normal, taking into consideration the fact that everyone is used to work with a group of people, is happy with his/ her success on the current job, etc. But, when the goals which are set in the career plan are not matching with the possibilities offered by the current job, a substantial reason for the change as mentioned above is being developed. Of course, this motivation should appear after all alternatives are eliminated: advancement, lateral moves, etc.

It is recommended that you don't drop your current job until you find a new one. I know it's hard to focus on both your current job and on the search process, too, but you should keep in mind that employers are not keen to hire unemployed people. Another obstacle, found by many individuals who are in job search process, is the difficulty of arranging interviews after the working program. But you need to take into consideration the breaks you have during your working program, too. Lunch break could be "your best friend" in this situation. Vacation days are also excellent for this purpose.

Keep in mind that your work performance at your current job should not be neglected. The apparent reason for the statement mentioned above comes from the fact that you don't want to lose your job until you find a new one. Other not-so-obvious reasons are related to the achievements that you need to learn continuously and the references from your real manager that could ease your hire on the new job.

When you are in the happy position of signing for the new job, leave your current organization in warm conditions, no matter what happened in the past and what you feel about certain colleagues/ managers in your department.

So, don't forget: look for a new job while you are still working on the current one; don't neglect your ongoing position; leave it on friendly terms.

• START YOUR OWN BUSINESS

Are you unsatisfied with your current job? If you are, you may be interested in changing employers. While it is more than possible for you to find, apply for, and be awarded a new job, did you know that is not your only option? Have you ever thought about starting your own business? If this is a thought that has yet to cross your mind, you may want give starting your own business some serious consideration. As nice as it is to hear that you should examine starting your own business, you may be curious as to which points you should take the time to examine. If you are serious about starting your own business or at least learning if running your own business is something that you are capable of doing, you will want to continue reading on.

A few important points that should be taken into consideration by those who are interested in leaving the traditional workplace to start a business are outlined below. One of the many points that you will want to take into consideration, when looking to start your own business, is the startup costs associated with doing so. Whether you would like to open up a gift shop or if you would like to sell your professional writing services, it is likely that you will need to make some startup purchases. The startup costs associated with starting your own business will all depend on the opportunities that you choose. Although there is likely to be some variance, it is likely that you will need to purchase a computer, internet service, a business phone, business phone service, a fax machine, a copier, an office desk, and other office furniture. If you have an ideal credit score, you may be able to receive financial assistance to get your business up and running. Another factor that you need to take into consideration, when looking to determine if you should leave your current job and start your own business is time.

Should you be interested in starting your own business, it is important to remember that you will likely not see success right away. Many businesses, no matter what the type, take time to see profits and success. You have to market your business to the general public, set up your online website or your storefront location, and do so much more. That is why it is important that you not only have enough money to get your business up and running, but you will also want to make sure that you also have enough money to support yourself and your family until you are able to start making a profit with your own business. Another one of the many factors that you will want to take into consideration, when trying to determine if you should start your own business, is insurance.

At your current position, do you have health insurance? If you are married, would you be able to get health insurance through your spouse? If you would be unable to do so, health insurance is something that you will want to take into consideration. Even if your health is fine right now, you never know what could happen, especially if your health insurance is also used to help cover the rest of your family. Should you decide to start your own business, you should be able to purchase insurance for yourself or for the rest of your family.

With that in mind, it is important to remember that insurance costs money, quite a bit of money to be exact. What is nice about starting your own business is that you, literally, have an unlimited number of options. For example, did you know that you can sell a product or a service? Popular startup businesses include gift shops, cleaning services, accounting services, and so forth. In addition to the type of business that you would like to start, you also have a number of different options when it comes to operating a business.

Many entrepreneurs run online businesses, storefront businesses, or even both. In all honesty, the decision is yours to make. With that in mind, the decisions that you do make can have a huge impact in determining whether or not your business, should you decide to start one, is a success.

Conclusion

Today every aspect has changed, and it is entirely different and much more complicated, due to the numerous and constant changes in economics and technology. It is quite clear that today a person must continuously acquire new skills, ability, and training throughout the whole working life. In short, career is a never-ending process, which is serene of the person working experience gained while performing different jobs and moving between the various positions, but it can also fulfill by achieving greater responsibility, skill, progression on his/her path of career.

The term career development is concerned with the potential of employees and the situation in which they are or may be at the moment and after that. Career development is vital to the individual employee. Career development is nothing but one's self-actualization, which contributes at the deepest level to working manner, motivation, and personal attainment, not only in the working life of an individual but also in the social sphere of individual's life.

Before starting developing his/her career, the individual has to make thorough consideration of possible solutions. Those answers merely imply all the connections and correlations between one's needs, ability and preferences, and the organization's capability, needs and conceivability.

Career development can be described as a term that has an integral focus and refers to the way an individual views his/her career but also has an external focus that relates to the series of jobs and positions held by an individual. Understanding career development requires an examination of two processes- how different plans and implement their career goals and how organization design and implement their career development programs.

Career affects both actors in the process of career development, an individual, and an organization, and it creates a relationship between them. So, career development is rather a complicated thing, divided into two important factors. Factors like, career planning, which represents employee's identification process and implements steps to attain career goals. The matching process is rather important, because of both, the individual and organization have their interests in individual's career.

Career planning also involves identifying the career -related goals and establishing plans for attaining these aims. It is a simple activity performed by an individual to understand and able to control their work life. To help you along this journey I have provided you a link to the "Couch to Career" Course (http://soldonsuccess.net/course/couch-to-career/). Use it help you through finding the career that is meant for you. The purpose is to find where you belong. It will be a road map to your success. Thank you for purchasing this book, I hope you will apply the acquired knowledge productively.

www.ingramcontent.com/pod-product-compliance
Lightning Source LLC
Chambersburg PA
CBHW061231180526
45170CB00003B/1254